This is my digger

Written by Chris Oxlade
Photography by Christine Lalla

SEA-TO-SEA
Mankato Collingwood London

This edition first published in 2008 by
Sea-to-Sea Publications
1980 Lookout Drive
North Mankato
Minnesota 56003

Printed in China

Library of Congress Cataloging in Publication Data

Oxlade, Chris.
    This is my digger / by Chris Oxlade.
        p.cm. -- (Mega machine drivers)
    ISBN 978-1-59771-104-3
    1. Earthmoving machinery--Juvenile literature. I. Title.

TA725.094 2007
621.8'65--dc22

                                    2006051278

9 8 7 6 5 4 3 2

Published by arrangement with the Watts Publishing Group Ltd, London.

Editor: Jennifer Schofield
Designer: Jemima Lumley
Photography: Christine Lalla
Digger driver: Andy Cook

Acknowledgments:
The Publisher would like to thank Karen Ross, Andy Cook,
and all at Diggerland for their help in producing this book.

Every attempt has been made to clear copyright.
Should there be any inadvertent omission please
apply to the publisher for rectification.

▶ Contents

My digger and me

Hello! I am a digger driver.
This is the digger that I drive.

My digger digs holes and picks up soil and rubble.

Digger power

This is my digger's engine.
It makes all the parts work.

The engine is under the cover.
It is big and powerful.

This is the fuel tank.
The engine needs fuel
to work.

Digger tracks

My digger has two tracks that move it backward and forward.

The tracks are made from thick, tough rubber.

The tracks are very wide to stop the digger from sinking into mud.

Boom and bucket

The boom makes the digging bucket move up and down.

bucket

boom

▷ *The bucket has teeth that dig into the ground.*

Rams move the boom up and down. They are like muscles that push and pull, just like in your arm.

ram

ram

Digger tools

I can put other tools onto the boom instead of the digging bucket.

A hammer breaks up rock and concrete.

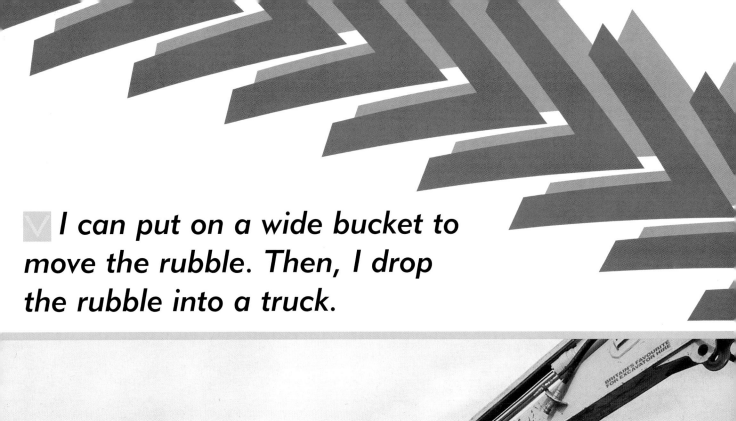

I can put on a wide bucket to move the rubble. Then, I drop the rubble into a truck.

In my cab

I sit in the cab to drive my digger.
The cab keeps me warm and dry.

The seat is comfortable and it is heated on cold days!

I can see the digger tools working through the big windows.

Digger controls

I drive the digger with pedals, levers, and switches.

The foot pedals make the tracks go forward and backward.

Hand levers work the boom and bucket. They also make the digger's body swing around.

Digging a hole

Today, my first job is to dig a hole on a construction site.

I make the bucket dig into the soil.

Then, I lift the bucket up and swing the body around.

I tip the bucket up to make the soil fall out.

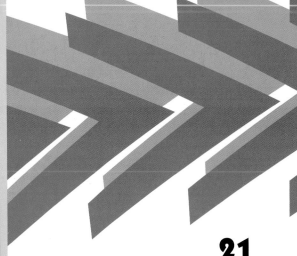

Breaking rocks

Now, I am using a bigger digger to break rocks and load a truck.

I am breaking up the rocks with the digger's hammer.

Then, I put a wide bucket onto the arm.

I use the bucket to load the rubble into a truck.

More diggers

Here are some more diggers that I drive.

This digger is called a backhoe loader. I use it to dig holes, lift heavy things, and move rubble.

I use this mini digger on sidewalks and in backyards.

Be a digger driver

It takes lots of practice
to become a digger driver.

*You have to learn how to drive the
digger safely around a construction site.*

You have to learn what all the digger's levers, pedals, and switches do.

You have to learn how to use all the different digger tools.

Digger parts

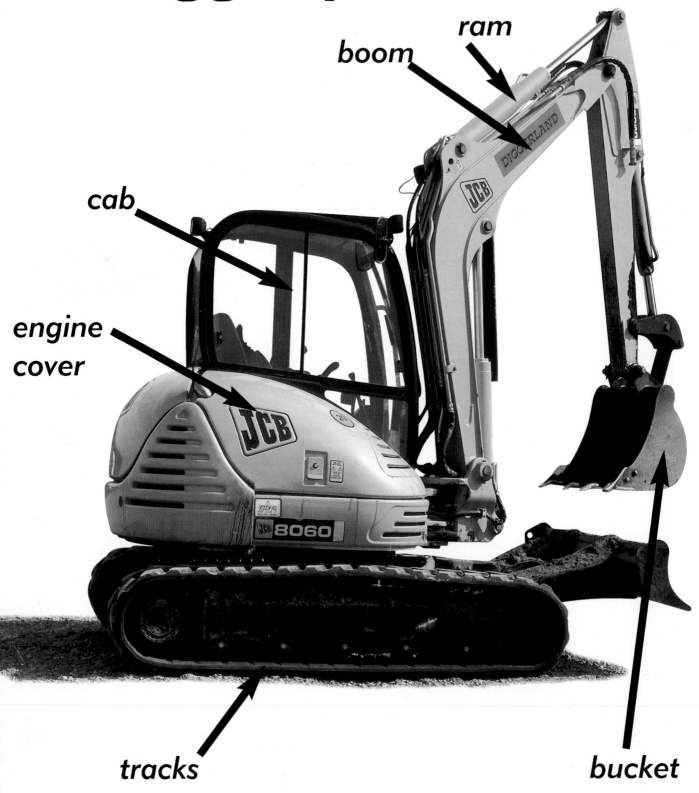

ram

boom

cab

engine
cover

bucket

tracks

Word bank

body—the main part of a digger

concrete—stone used in buildings

construction site—the place where a building is built

engine—the part of a digger that makes it move

fuel—the liquid that burns inside an engine

mini—small

rubble—pieces of stone

tools—the things, such as buckets and hammers, that are added to a digger to do different jobs

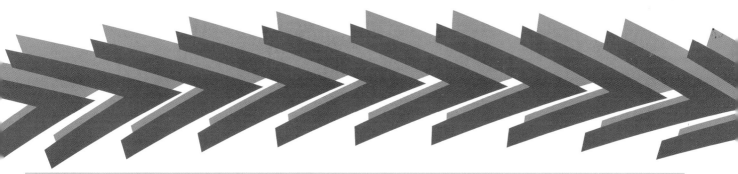

Web fun

Look at JCB's children's website for loads of digger fun:
www.jcb.com/(wpjfrg45paq2ju55udsxlmyp)/jcbjunior/index.aspx

Index